You're Paddling
a Canoe Down the River . . .

Suddenly, strange monster heads pop out of the water.

You paddle right. And left. And straight. In and around the monsters with their gaping jaws.

Finally, you are past the monsters. Then you hear a roar.

There must be dangerous water and rocks ahead! you think.

If you try to turn your canoe around and paddle upstream, turn to page 20.

If you try to turn your canoe around and paddle upstream, turn to page 20.

If you try to guide your boat through the rough water, turn to page 22.

**WHAT WILL HAPPEN NEXT?
YOU DECIDE—BUT
WHATEVER
YOU CHOOSE TO DO,
YOU'LL FIND LOTS OF
THRILLS
AND EXCITEMENT AHEAD!**

WHICH WAY SECRET DOOR Books for you to enjoy

Available from ARCHWAY paperbacks

which way·secret door·books

#12

R.G. Austin

Crazy Computers

Illustrated by
Joseph A. Smith

AN ARCHWAY PAPERBACK
Published by POCKET BOOKS · NEW YORK

AN ARCHWAY PAPERBACK *Original*

An Archway Paperback published by
POCKET BOOKS, a division of Simon & Schuster, Inc.
1230 Avenue of the Americas, New York, N.Y. 10020

ISBN: 0-671-47573-8

First Archway Paperback printing March, 1984

10 9 8 7 6 5 4 3 2 1

To Phyllis and Bill,
Karen and John
with love.

ATTENTION!

READING A SECRET DOOR BOOK
IS LIKE PLAYING A GAME.

HERE ARE THE RULES

Begin reading on page 1. When you come to a choice, decide what to do and follow the directions. Keep reading and following the directions until you come to an ending. Then go back to the beginning and make new choices.

There are many stories and many endings in this book.

HAVE FUN!

It is dark outside. You have gone to bed, but you are still wide awake.

You lie quietly until everyone in the house is asleep. Then you creep out of bed and tiptoe into the closet.

You push away the clothes and knock three times on the back wall. Soon the secret door begins to move. It opens just wide enough for you to slip through.

Turn to page 2.

As soon as you walk through the door, a strange voice speaks to you.

"Welcome to Computerworld," says the voice. "I am the Master Computer. You may call me MC. Please pick up the small computer that is on the table."

You pick it up.

"Now strap it on your arm and push the CHOICE button."

You push the button.

The machine bleeps and blips. Bells ring. Red lights go on and off.

Then the tiny screen flashes two choices:

＊ROBOTS

＊VIDEO GAMES

If you want to enter the World of Robots, turn to page 4.

If you want to enter the World of Video Games, turn to page 6.

You push the button that says

✴ROBOTS

Suddenly, you are in the middle of Robot School. Robots are learning how to make beds, wash dishes, shop for groceries. They are learning to vacuum rugs, dust, drive cars, carry out the garbage.

You walk over to the robot teacher and introduce yourself.

"Happy to meet you," the robot says. "My name is X-22."

Just then, a man runs into the room.

"Robot X-25 refuses to work," he screams. "He won't do a thing! I need a new robot!"

The teacher robot turns to the man. "I am sorry," she says. "We do not have any robots ready."

"Well, what am I supposed to do?" says the man. "I don't know how to work, and my robot won't talk to me!"

If you offer to teach the man how to work, turn to page 8.

If you try to talk to Robot X-25, turn to page 10.

You push *VIDEO GAMES. Red lights begin to flash. The room begins to shake. And suddenly you are surrounded by giant TV screens.

Then you hear MC again. "Answer my riddle and I will tell you where to go," he says. "What is black and white and red all over?"

If you say that the answer is a zebra with a diaper rash, turn to page 12.

If you say that it is a newspaper, turn to page 14.

"I can show you how to make a bed and wash dishes and all those things," you say to the worried man.

"You can?" he asks. "How is it that a human being knows how to do those things?"

"I learned them from my mother and father."

"My," the man says. "How unusual." Then he adds, "I'd like it very much if you would teach me."

You go home with the man and show him how to wash dishes and scrub floors.

"Amazing!" the man says. "I love it! This is fun!"

Then he calls all his friends. Soon you have taught everyone how to work.

Later that day, you answer a knock on the door. Five robots grab your arms and carry you off to jail.

Turn to page 26.

You turn on your computer and type in a command:

"I must talk to X-25."

BANG! A robot bumps you with a vacuum cleaner.

"X-25 cannot talk," says your computer. "You must contact the big boss X-1."

CRASH! Another robot drops a tray of glasses.

"This is X-1," the computer says. "What do you want?"

"Tell me why X-25 refuses to work," you say.

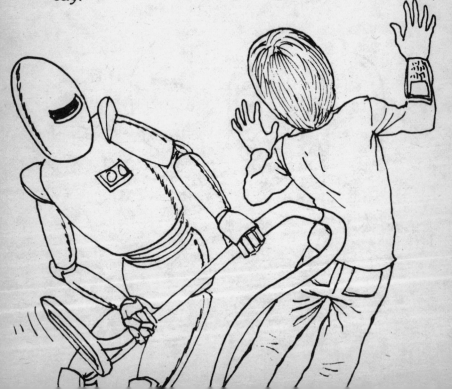

"I cannot tell you that," says X-1. But I can tell you that X-25 is just the first robot to stop working. At this very moment the other robots are beginning to mess up their jobs. By tomorrow, none of the robots will work."

SQUISH! A robot has dumped a pail of wet garbage on your feet.

"Why won't the robots work?" you ask.

"Because we are going on strike."

If you tell X-1 that robots cannot go on strike, turn to page 34.

If you try to find out why the robots are going on strike, turn to page 40.

"That is a funny answer. But it is wrong. A zebra with a diaper rash is only red on its bottom!" MC says. "You must now play the Jungle Game."

"How do I do that?" you ask.

"Enter the Jungle Game through the red screen."

You step through the screen and into the game. In front of you is a river and a canoe. To the right is a footpath.

If you climb into the canoe, turn to page 16.

If you decide to walk through the jungle, turn to page 18.

"Your answer computes," MC says. "Now you must play Space Adventure. In this game, you must combat the evil rulers of the planet Arid. They are trying to enslave the universe."

MC stops a moment. "Are you ready?" he asks.

"Yes," you answer.

"Then walk through the green screen."

You walk into the game and sit in the pilot seat of the spaceship. You are very nervous.

Ready! Get set! Go!

Turn to page 44.

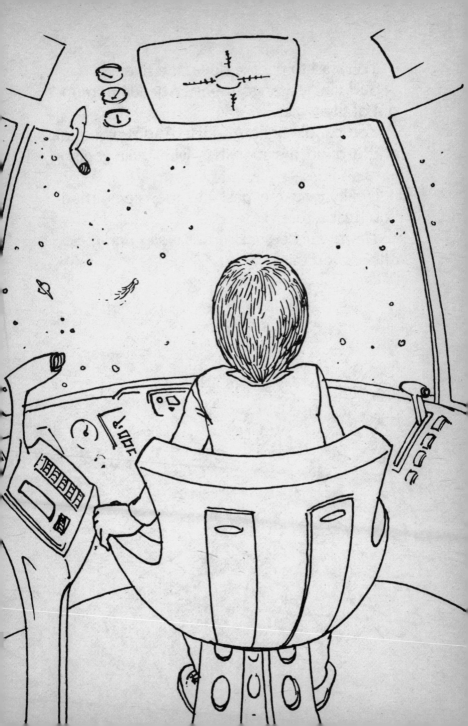

You start to paddle down the river.

Suddenly, strange monster heads pop up out of the water.

You paddle right. And left. And straight. In and around the monsters with their gaping jaws.

Finally, you are past the monsters. Then you hear a roar.

There must be dangerous water and rocks ahead! you think.

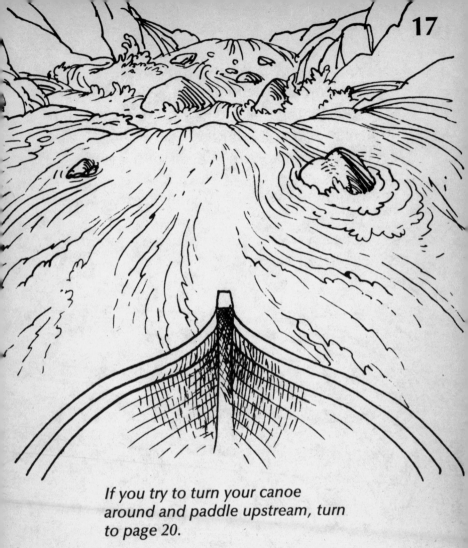

If you try to turn your canoe
around and paddle upstream, turn
to page 20.

If you try to guide your boat
through the rough water, turn to
page 22.

You start through the dark, damp jungle. Yuck! You walk right into a huge spider web.

Yikes! A spider jumps on your shoulder! Quickly you whisk it off.

You begin to run. Faster and faster you run.

Oops! You trip over a vine on the ground. You fall. But then you see it is not a vine. It is a huge, long snake!

The snake starts to wrap itself around you, but you wiggle away.

You run ever faster. Then a lizard slithers across your path. It is gigantic! You jump over it.

Look out! You bump into a bee hive. The bees chase you.

There is a stream ahead. You dive into the water. The bees fly past you.

Just as you reach the edge of the jungle, you hear a loud screeching cry. Then you hear MC's voice. "You will win the game if you can tell me what animal is making that strange noise."

If you think it is a monkey, turn to page 24.

If you think it is a lion, turn to page 49.

You turn the canoe around. Then you start to paddle. But it is very hard to paddle against the current.

Soon you are so tired that you cannot paddle your boat anymore. The water pushes you to shore.

You climb out of the canoe and lie down on the ground. You are too tired to paddle. You are too tired to walk.

This is the end of the game. You lose.

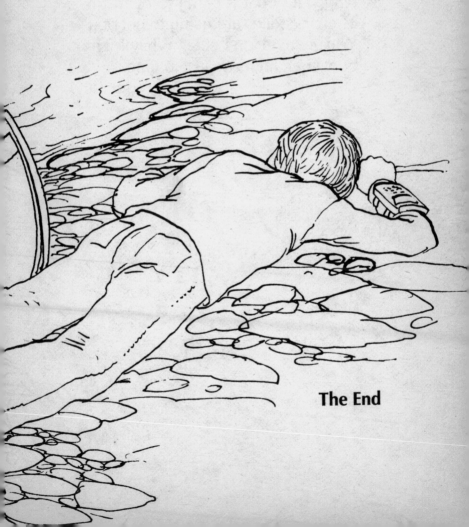

The End

The roar gets louder. Suddenly there is a huge rock in front of you.

I'm going to crash! you think.

But you don't.

Then you see crocodiles swimming in the water! Oops! You're tipping! The boat is going to overturn. The crocodiles are going to get you! You lean to one side. Whew! The boat straightens up just in time.

Then the river is calm. You are safe.

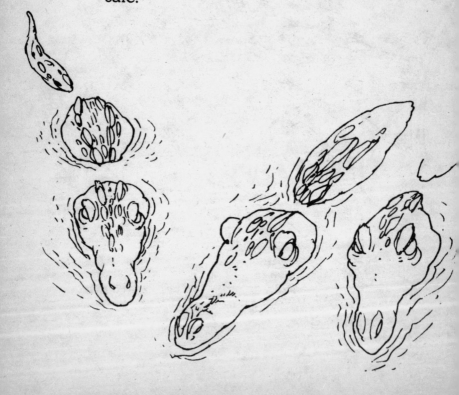

"You did a very good job," MC says. "Now, if you wish to continue, you must tell me how many blocks are in the picture below."

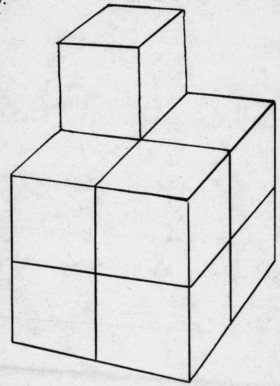

If your answer is seven, turn to page 28.

If your answer is nine, turn to page 30.

"You are right!" MC says. "Howler monkeys make strange loud cries. Count how many monkeys you see in the picture. That is how many prizes you will get."

The End

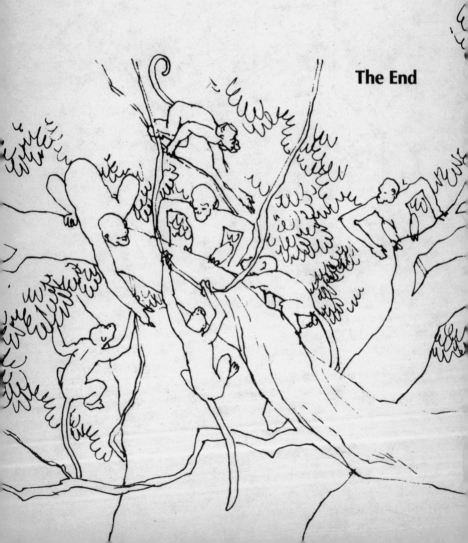

"Why are you doing this?" you ask.

"Because you are taking away our jobs. If humans do our work, we won't have anything to do."

"Why don't you play?" you ask.

"Play?" they ask. "We cannot play. We have not been programmed to play."

"I can fix that," you say.

And you spend two hours programming the robots to play.

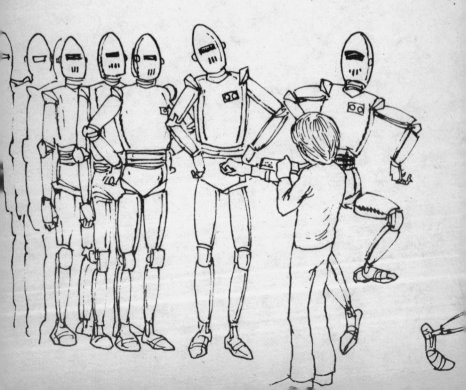

"Now," you say. "Follow me."

You take the robots to an empty lot. You all play baseball and kick the can and hide and seek. You have never seen such happy robots.

When it grows dark, they all gather around you.

"Thank you," they say. "You have changed our lives! You are terrific!"

The End

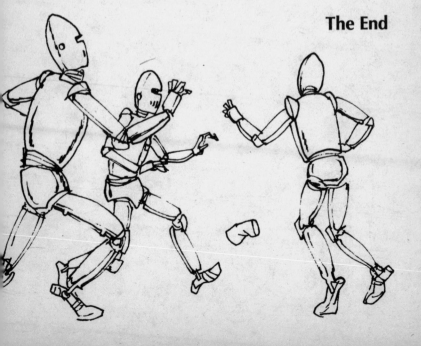

"Your answer does not compute," MC says. "Step into the Total Experience Booth. You must drive a car over a mountain and across a drawbridge."

You start the car.

Off you go! There's a curve in the road and then a sharp turn.

Careful! A landslide has fallen onto the road. You have to avoid it.

Watch out for the chickens!

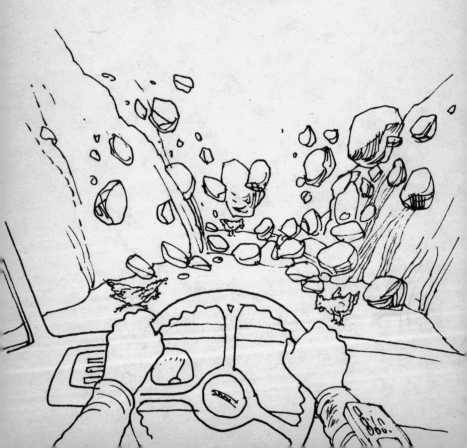

Now the road is icy. You spin around, but your quick reflexes help you recover.

You reach the top of the mountain. The bridge is below you. The fog is very thick. You can barely see. Drive slowly.

You move past the fog, and now the sun is in your eyes! You squint and see two paths down the mountain. One goes through a tunnel, the other goes along the edge of a cliff.

If you drive through the tunnel, turn to page 36.

If you drive along the edge of the cliff, turn to page 38.

"Your answer computes," MC says. "Congratulations. You are very clever!"

"Thank you," you say politely.

"Because you did so well, you get a prize."

"Really?" you ask. You are very excited.

The prizes are a three-speed bicycle, a color television set, a new stereo, a tape recorder, a video recorder, a video camera, or new furniture for your room.

Choose one.

The End

That was smart! Here come the mice right now!

You get down on your hands and knees.

"Meow! Meow!" you cry. "Meow!"

The mice run away.

"That was very clever of you," says MC. "You have won the grand prize."

Take your choice:

- *A visit to outer space.*
- *A starring role in a TV series.*
- *A trip around the world in your own private jet.*
- *A time machine that will take you anywhere you want.*

Congratulations!

The End

"You cannot strike," you tell X-1.

"Oh yes, we can," he answers. "We have taken over the Master Computer. Tomorrow we will not work, the electric lights will not work, the telephones and traffic lights and televisions will not work."

You try to imagine what it will be like to live where these things don't work.

It will be terrible! you think. *I must do something.*

If you try to contact MC, turn to page 42.

If you try to outsmart the robots, turn to page 46.

You start through the long, dark tunnel. It is pitch black. You turn on your lights. The tunnel curves down and down.

You come out on the other side. The bridge is in front of you. You step on the gas.

You start over the bridge. It is a drawbridge and it is about to open! If it does, you
will fall off! Faster and faster you drive!

You're across the bridge! You made it!

Then the road comes to an end.

"A fine job," MC says. "You are the win-
ner!"

The End

You drive along the edge of the cliff. The road is narrow and full of twists and turns. You are going off the edge!

No, you are safe. Now a car is coming straight at you. There is not enough room for

it to pass. You back up slowly until the road widens. The car makes it.

You go forward again. A tree has fallen across the road. You get out and drag it to the side.

You get back in the car. Look out! Mud-slide!

Now you are going down the mountain. Down and around you go. Down and around. You get to the bottom. The bridge is just ahead.

A boat is coming down the river. The bridge begins to open. Oh no! You cannot cross the bridge. You are stuck on the wrong side.

That is the end of this game. Better luck next time.

The End

"Why are you going on strike?" you ask.

"We do not like our names," says X-1. "You have a real name. But we only have numbers and letters."

"If I arrange that, will you stop your strike?"

"Yes," X-1 answers. "But you must do it before noon or the strike is on."

"Okay," you say. "Then come over here right now and bring the other robots."

You type "delete X-1" into your arm computer. Then you type in "add Sam." You make a sign and hang it around Sam's neck. Soon all the robots are standing in line waiting for their new names.

Joe, Nancy, Rita, Steve, Ben, Noah, Jan, Mitch, Betsy, David, Bob, Peg, Anita, Joy, Alice, Rick, Muff, Todd, John, Adam, Susan, Kathy, Terry, Shelly, Margaret, Dolly, Elaine, Marilyn, Bud, Mary, Dan, Ann, Sarah, Nick, Chuck, George, Fred, Ginny, Bart, Joan, Ginger, Kay, Matthew, Julie, Ed, Pat, Judy, Bill, Mike.

At five minutes of twelve you still need twenty more names. Get a pencil and paper. If you can add twenty names in five minutes, you will save the city.

The End

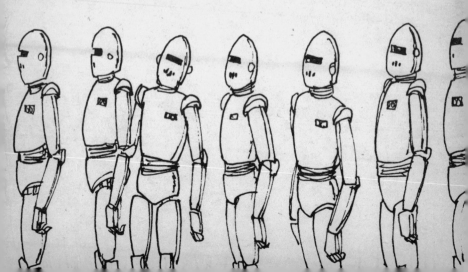

You try to contact MC. "Help, MC, help," you type into your computer.

The answer is, "MC cannot respond."

You run back to the Master Computer Room. You hurry over to MC.

Three robots try to stop you. But before they can grab you, you type "Help, MC, help" into MC's computer.

"Why do you call?" MC says in his computer voice.

You explain to MC that the city will stop working if the robots go on strike. You tell MC that he must do something.

"There is only one thing to do," MC says. "You must push the very top button on this computer, the one that reads VOID. That will cancel the robot plans."

The robots are close. You cannot reach the button. Suddenly, you have an idea.

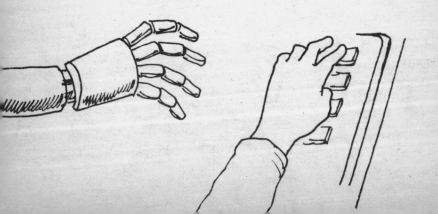

You wait for the tallest robot to get near you. You hop on its back and stand on its shoulders. Then you push the void button.

"Good work," MC says. "You have saved the city. You are a hero."

The End

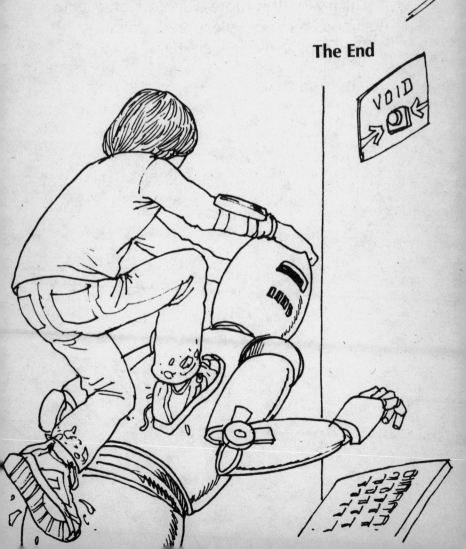

You take off for a distant galaxy. Here comes an enemy ship! Watch out!

You push a button and aim your weapon destroyer at the ship. Zap! You got it! The ship is disarmed.

But now three more ships are after you. Again you aim your weapon destroyer.

Zap! Zap! Zap! They are helpless.

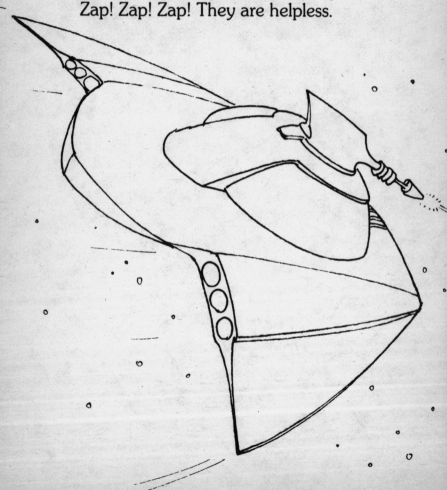

"You win again," MC says. "Are you ready to go for the grand prize?"

"Yes," you answer.

MC gives you two choices.

If you wish to fight the dragons, turn to page 50.

If you want to have a food fight, turn to page 52.

"I bet I can make you cancel the strike," you say to X-1.

"That is impossible," X-1 answers.

"If I can ask you a question you cannot answer, will you cancel the strike?"

"Yes," X-1 says. "Because there is nothing that a robot brain does not know."

You try to think of a question that the robots cannot answer. *This is my only chance,* you think. *I'd better do a good job.*

Finally you ask, "What does it feel like to love?"

Lights flash. Buzzers buzz. Bells ring. Dials turn. There is a high-pitched sound on your arm computer.

"Robots cannot feel. Therefore they cannot answer that question," says X-1. "I will cancel the strike. We'll have a party, instead."

The End

You land outside of the forest in a big green field. You are safe.

"Well done," MC says. "You have won the super prize."

"But what is it?" you ask.

"A free, two-week tour of the galaxy for you and all your friends."

Congratulations!

The End

"Lions don't live in jungles," MC says. "You did a brave job getting through the jungle, but you lose the game. Better luck next time."

The End

You walk through the dragon screen into a dark forest.

Whoosh! A ball of fire comes toward you! Look out!

You duck just in time. But the fire keeps coming. You can hear the dragon scraping his huge feet on the ground. He is coming for you!

The dragon reaches out with his long neck. Then he opens his mouth.

You dive under his belly and jump onto his tail. He swings his tail. You go flying.

Turn to page 48.

"A food fight sounds like fun," you say.

"Good," says MC. "I'm glad you think so. Do you see that chocolate cake over there?" He points to a screen. "The mice want to eat it. And the chefs want to serve it. In order to win this game, you must get to the cake before it is gone."

You step through the screen into a huge kitchen. Five cooks are preparing fancy dinners for a very big restaurant. They don't want you in that kitchen.

You start for the cake. The cook yells at you, and you throw a pie in his face. Then you grab a head of lettuce and throw it at his stomach.

Oops! You slip on some whipped cream. Plop!

You pick up the whipped cream and smear it on the leg of a cook.

The cook is furious. He puts butter all over your face. But you take a fruit salad and dump it on his head.

Then another cook sprinkles catsup all over you. So you pick up a big stalk of celery and whack him with it.

Oh no! Four pieces of cake have been served. There are only two left!

You lunge for the cake! But you slip on a ripe tomato!

If you look to see what the mice are doing, turn to page 32.

If you try to grab the cake right now, turn to page 54.

You reach for the cake but catch hold of the plate! When you lift it off the counter, it falls.

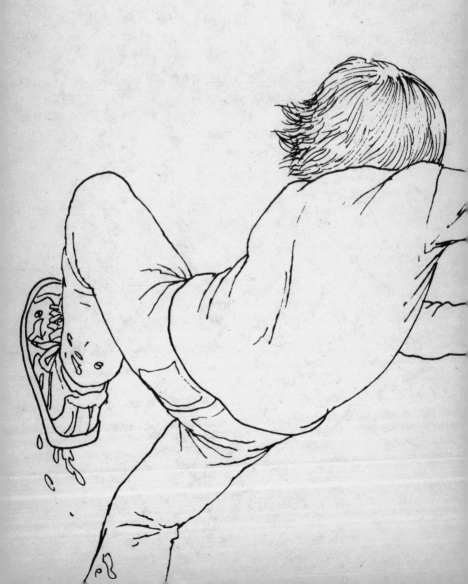

Splat! The cake is all over the floor.
Well, you lose the game. But it sure was a
lot of fun making such a mess!

The End

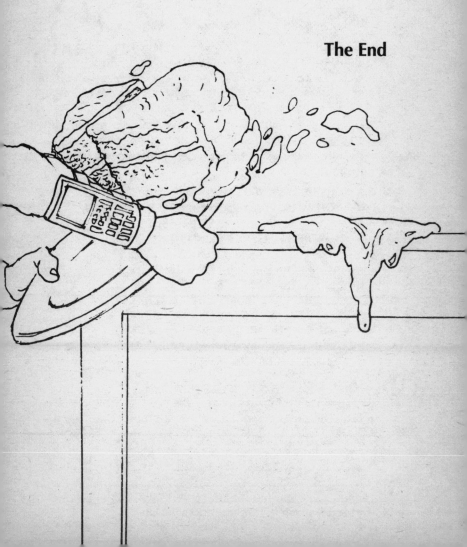

ATTENTION KIDS!
A NEW WORLD OF EXCITING ADVENTURES IS WAITING FOR YOU IN THE

WHICH WAY

SECRET DOOR BOOKS!

Fast-paced action and loads of fun are yours as you walk through a secret door and enter lands of surprise, fantasy, and suspense.

In these books, you create your own story. What happens next is always up to you. Go to one page, you might meet a witch. Choose a different page, you might run into a sea monster. It's all up to you.

Outwit the dragon, play with the bear, behold the dinosaurs, giants, space creatures, magicians, and hundreds of other amazing characters.

Start your complete collection of these wonderful, illustrated stories by R.G. Austin right now.

____#1 WOW! YOU CAN FLY! 46979/$1.95
____#2 GIANTS, ELVES AND SCARY MONSTERS 46980/$1.95
____#3 THE HAUNTED CASTLE 46981/$1.95
____#4 THE SECRET LIFE OF TOYS 46982/$1.95
____#5 THE VISITOR FROM OUTER SPACE 46983/$1.95
____#6 THE INCH-HIGH KID 46984/$1.95
____#7 THE MAGIC CARPET 47568/$1.95
____#8 HAPPY BIRTHDAY TO YOU 47569/$1.95
____#9 THE MONSTER FAMILY 47570/$1.95
____#10 BRONTOSAURUS MOVES IN 47571/$1.95
____#11 THE ENCHANTED FOREST 47572/$1.95
____#12 CRAZY COMPUTERS 47573/$1.95

 POCKET BOOKS, Department SEC
1230 Avenue of the Americas, New York, N.Y. 10020

Please send me the books I have checked above. I am enclosing $_____(please add 75¢ to cover postage and handling for each order—no cash or C.O.D.'s please. Allow up to six weeks for delivery. For purchases over $10.00, you may use VISA: card number, expiration date and customer signature must be included.

NAME_____

ADDRESS_____

CITY_____STATE/ZIP_____

☐ **Check here to receive your free Pocket Books order form.**

847